Dudley the Angel and His Buddy Gabby the Elf

Manuel James Birch

Illustrated by Lisa Thompson Ahnen

AuthorHouse™
1663 Liberty Drive
Bloomington, IN 47403
www.authorhouse.com
Phone: 833-262-8899

This book is printed on acid-free paper.

ISBN: 978-1-4490-1704-0 (sc)
ISBN: 978-1-4634-6468-4 (e)

Library of Congress Control Number: 2009908550

Print information available on the last page.

Published by AuthorHouse 09/14/2022

authorHOUSE®

My grandchildren Raace and Caleb were my inspiration.

They are two of the brightest lights in my life.

ABOUT THE AUTHOR

The author's first book, a novella called Snow Angels and the Two Pearls, was published in 2005. The inspiration for writing a children's book was manifested by watching his two grandsons play, listening to their stories, and being introduced to their imaginary friends.

The author resides in Scottsdale, Arizona.

Chapter 1
Hello

Hello, kids! My name is Gabby the elf.

I am a Christmas elf. My best buddy's name is Dudley. He is a Christmas angel. Dudley has a problem and needs our help. Dudley cannot land in a Christmas tree without crashing. We need to help Dudley land and pass his flight school.

Once he passes his tests, he will have a very important mission. This mission will change the life of a family in a fantastic way! There is a lot to do, and I need your help. Working together, we will help Dudley create a miracle … a Christmas miracle.

Oh, if you do not listen to my story, I have a warning. I will pull your ears. If your mom or dad does not listen, you might have to pull their ears.

Did I tell you that mothers of angels do not like elves? They think we play tricks and are just naughty. Well, children, elves are not naughty; we just have magical powers and we like to have fun!

Now are you ready to help Dudley?

I can't hear you!

Oh, that's better!

Chapter 2
Rise and Shine

"Dudley, wake up. Wake up, you sleepyhead. It is time for you to get ready for flight school," Dudley's angel mother said, standing over him.

"Oh, Mom, do I have to? I don't want to."

"Yes, you have to!"

"Why? I have already been in flight school for almost 2,000 years!" Dudley was not happy.

"Dudley, it has been exactly 1,995 years, 11 months, 23 days, and 2 minutes. Your dad's heavenly credit card is maxed out to pay for your flight school. You must pass the test today. Christmas is almost here."

"It is not my fault, Mom. There are those angels who just don't like me because of my one small mistake many years ago. I thought angels always forgive and forget. They don't. They never forgive. They never forget. I think I'll just skip flight school today. I will make the perfect landing tomorrow."

"Get your stuff together," she said. "Get ready for school. Now!"

"Do I have to?" He made a very sad face.

Dudley very slowly put one foot out of his cloud. He said in a very loud voice, "I need a new halo and wand to bring the miracle of Christmas to a special family. This stuff is no good. The reason I am failing in flight school is that I need some new stuff."

Dudley's mother looked at him. "Dudley, go to school now!"

"Okay." Dudley hung his head. "I must pass my test, I must pass my test."

Mother remembered a phone call from before. "Your elf friend called. Can't you find an *angel* friend? You know how I feel about elves. The elf-angel convention this year was a mess. Your elf friends threw frozen yogurt balls at everyone, and that pet troll popped out of our angel food cake. Well, they were just naughty. Find a *new* friend."

Dudley softly said, "You just don't understand me. Gabby is my bud."

"Well, find a new bud." Mother knew Dudley was sad, but she also knew Gabby's friendship was not right for her son. Gabby was trouble!

Dudley was scared to leave.

Poor Dudley. He needs some good luck today.

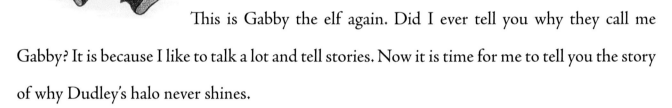

This is Gabby the elf again. Did I ever tell you why they call me Gabby? It is because I like to talk a lot and tell stories. Now it is time for me to tell you the story of why Dudley's halo never shines.

Many years ago, all the angels were asked to visit a special child who was born in a manger far, far away. A very bright star was shining down upon a little town to guide the angels to see: the first miracle of Christmas.

Dudley just wanted a closer look at the little boy in the cradle, but he crashed into a stack of hay, scaring all of the animals and knocking down three very nice men in long robes. The angels were very upset, and from that day on, they would never let Dudley forget his mistake.

Now we need to cheer for Dudley! Can you cheer and say "Dudley!"?

I didn't hear you. You didn't cheer loud enough.

One more time! Okay. That is better.

I gotta run. Santa Claus is calling for me. I need to get back to work making toys for Christmas. See ya!

"Dudley?"

"Yes, Mom?"

"It is December 23. You only have one more chance to pass flight school." She tried to smile but could not hide her doubt.

Dudley looked at his mother, hung his head, and walked out. Three angels with golden wings met him and shouted, "There's Crash Dudley. Dudley, what are you doing today, crashing on your halo? Crash Dudley! Crash Dudley!"

In a very loud voice, Dudley said, "I must pass my test."

Chapter 3
Flight School

Dudley sat at the back of the class. His wings drooped. He hated the name "Crash Dudley." The angel flight leader stood at the head of the class.

"You all know you must pass this test today or you will not deliver a miracle of Christmas to your special family. Flight Leader looked directly at Dudley. "Some of you must try even harder."

Dudley whispered, "I'll try to pass my test. I'll ..." He then remembered what his good friend Gabby the Elf said, 'You must say, *I will pass my test*.'

Dudley thought again, and softly said, "I *will* pass my test. I will!"

Flight Leader said in a booming voice, "Listen to me, angel cadets. You will be given a test Christmas tree. Dudley, your Christmas tree is number ten. You are cleared for takeoff."

Dudley took a deep breath and wasted not another moment. He took off and started to fly down toward the tree. He began to wobble. His wings started to flutter. He took a left turn around the star, just missing it. He slipped between two large Christmas ornament balls. The icicles on the tree began to shake. *Oh, not again. Please, not another bad landing. No!* He felt his ears being pulled very hard. His landing was perfect. All the decorations were still on the tree. Dudley had passed his test. Dudley felt his ears being pulled again, but thought, *Gabby can't be here. Angels are invisible, not elves.*

Dudley stood very proudly before the angel flight leader. "Dudley, you have passed your test." The leader then presented him with his golden wings, magic wand, and shiny halo. Dudley jumped up and down! He must tell Mom and Dad he passed his test! Tomorrow he would bring a miracle of Christmas to a special family.

It's Gabby again. I am so proud of Dudley! Remember how positive he was? He said, "I *will* pass my test." It is not enough to *try* to do something. You have to be sure in your heart that you *will* get it done. I was very excited. I called Dudley's home. His mother answered the phone, and when she figured out it was me, she hung up. I don't understand it; I'm so lovable. I still have to win her over. Maybe candy would help.

"Mom! Mom! I passed my test!" Dudley said. "I have my golden wings, miracle wand, and new shiny halo! I am going to bring the miracle of Christmas to a special family. Aren't you proud of me, Mom?"

"I am very happy and proud of you, son. If you want me to stay happy, please find a new friend. Elves make me nervous, and you can do better than Gabby."

"But Mom, Gabby helped me pass my test. He is my bud. I think he pulled on my ears. That is why I landed in the tree. I didn't knock one decoration off."

"Elves can't do that." Mother was tired of talking about Gabby.

"I don't know how he did it, but he did," Dudley said.

"Dudley, you passed your test. That is wonderful. I will call your father. He will be very proud of you. It has been a long day. I still want you to find a new friend."

Dudley smiled and quietly hoped that his mother will someday like Gabby. If she ever did, that might be a miracle of its own.

Chapter 4
A Very Special Christmas Family

Hi, it's Gabby, and welcome to chapter 4! We're moving right along.

Now it is time to introduce you to our new friends, Alex and Emmy. Alex and Emmy's family came to the United States only one year ago. They left because of trouble in their home country.

They live in a very small town called Nothing, Arizona. No, really. It is called Nothing. Alex and Emmy are going to have their first Christmas in their new home, in their new country of America.

"Momma, I miss Grandma and Grandpa. I miss the farm and the Christmas cookies," Alex said. His heart felt heavy.

"Alex, I will make you yummy cookies like I used to."

"Do you miss Grandma and Grandpa?" he asked his mother.

"Yes," she said. "And the old country too." Momma kept a small smile, being strong for her son. "When I look at the Christmas tree, I think about our old home."

"Momma, why did those people burn our house?" Alex asked.

"I don't know. They were bad people."

"Momma?"

"Yes, Alex?"

"Why did we run to the mountains?"

"So you and Emmy would be safe." She did not like to talk about the trouble, but she knew Alex needed to.

"Will people burn our house in America?"

"No, Alex."

He smiled. "Oh, Momma, do you remember the American soldier who found us? He gave us chocolates and took us to a safe place. He was a nice soldier. I think I understand now what he told me. He said, *Merry Christmas.*"

"I wish Grandma and Grandpa could be here. Will we ever see them again?" Alex asked, close to tears.

"I do not know, Alex. We can only hope."

Alex hugged his momma and left the kitchen to go to the Christmas tree.

Moments later, Momma heard a muffled giggle from her two children in the front room. She smiled and said, "Children, stop peeking at the Christmas presents."

"Momma, we are not peeking," Emmy replied.

"Then what is going on in there?" Momma walked into the room.

Emmy was standing by the Christmas tree with her fingers in her mouth. Alex was looking with a blank stare at the tree. There were ornament balls lying on the floor everywhere.

Emmy, in her very small voice, said, "Momma, I didn't do it, I didn't do it," as she looked at her older brother.

Alex chimed in, "Momma, I didn't do it. I was just standing here, and all the decorations fell off the Christmas tree."

"Alex, Emmy, go play somewhere else. I will put the ornaments back when I finish the cookies. Now, go!"

Children, did you hear that? Alex and Emmy did not knock those decorations off the tree! In your house, sometimes balls fall off the Christmas tree, right? And you didn't do it. I'll tell you a secret, but you cannot tell anyone, because this is an extra-special secret between children and elves. Christmas elves have fun and knock ornaments off of trees. It's fun to do! Alex and Emmy didn't knock the balls off of the Christmas tree. They fell off of the tree because the elves and trolls had a Christmas ball fight.

Now here is a *bigger secret!* I have invisible elf dust for all of us! You can come with me, but the big people need to stay at home. Now you can call me Captain Gabby! Kids, are you ready to go on our mission?

We must keep the decorations on the tree for Dudley when he lands, and I need extra elf dust for the troll to hold the star.

Now Dudley is ready to leave flight school.

Dudley stood in front of his flight leader at attention, listening carefully for his instructions. Flight Leader spoke in a very loud voice. "Dudley, your first assignment is a family in Nothing, Arizona."

"Nothing, Arizona? Where is Nothing?" This sounded funny to Dudley.

"It is your job to find it, Dudley. Don't mess it up." Flight Leader was hiding a smile.

"Yes, I will make a perfect landing and bring a miracle of Christmas to this family."

"Dudley, we hope so." Flight Leader and the rest of his classmates stood and clapped for their newest flyer, Dudley.

Chapter 5
Christmas Eve

Alex and Emmy's poppa and momma finally had a moment to sit together in their new little home. Poppa was eating one of his Santa cookies and drinking a cup of hot apple cider. He took a piece of mistletoe from his pocket and held it over Momma's head. "Momma, you are under the mistletoe. Give me a Christmas kiss."

The children, Alex and Emmy, giggled as they walked into the room and saw their parents kissing.

Poppa laughed and told the little spies that it was time for bed.

"We're too excited to sleep!" Emmy squealed.

"I am starving. I am too hungry to sleep," Alex said.

Momma laughed. "Alex, you ate cookies faster than I could bake them."

"Now go to sleep!" Poppa's order brought hugs from Alex and Emmy. In just moments, the children were in their beds. They closed their eyes, waiting for sleep, Santa Claus, Christmas, and for wishes to come true.

In the night sky high above, Dudley saw a small light and reported to Flight Leader, "This is Dudley. I have found Nothing."

"Nothing? Nothing? Keep looking." This could get confusing.

"Nothing, Arizona. It is a small place and there is only one light on. Oh, yes! I can see a little Christmas tree in the window. That is it. It's my Christmas miracle home."

Flight Leader took a deep breath. "Keep your approach steady and don't crash, Dudley."

Dudley was now coming in on his final approach. There was no place to land. He made another circle, but he still could not find a place to land. He was starting to shake and wobble. Then he felt his ears being pulled. He thought, *Is that you, Gabby?*

Dudley crashed into the tree. He hit several Christmas balls and landed on his head, but not one ball fell off. He thought he heard giggles all around him, but no one was there. He looked on the floor and saw there were no balls, no tinsel, just Christmas presents neatly stacked under the tree. "I did it!"

Momma and Poppa sat looking at the tree, and then their eyes closed. Poppa held Momma's hands; he had a little smile on his face. For Dudley, the moment had finally come to bring a miracle of Christmas to this family who had come from far away to live in America. Dudley shook his wand, waving it twice.

Momma and Poppa's eyes fluttered. They both fell fast asleep and hours passed in a moment. In their deep sleep, they were now both standing in their former country. The parents were sharing the dream. They were there together. They could see their old home, their neighbors, the sights and sounds of the country before they lost them to the trouble.

They saw their parents. Grandpa and Grandma were there too. Smiling, healthy, happy in this dream, the grandparents looked like they did before the bad people took them, before they went missing and were feared gone forever.

Through the happy dream came the voices of Alex and Emmy. They were excited; they had discovered a tree surrounded by presents and their parents on the couch together.

Momma and Poppa slowly woke to find Alex and Emmy very happy after a good night's sleep. In the children's excitement, the knock at the door was hard to hear. Then came another knock.

It surprised the parents. They all knew so few people in America. Who could be at the door this early Christmas morning?

Through the glass of the door, the family could only see the outline, the shadow of three people.

"I'll get it," Poppa said. He got up and moved toward the door. He had a strong feeling in his stomach. Momma was feeling the same thing, a kind of fear and happiness mixed together.

Poppa opened the door and his heart almost stopped. An officer with the United States Army stood on his doorstep. He smiled and stepped to the side to reveal Grandma and Grandpa standing before him.

Momma jumped up and was at the door without touching the floor. Grandma and Grandpa walked in, and the family was together for the first time in years. They covered each other with so many hugs and tears of joy.

The army officer explained that Grandma and Grandpa had been taken away and put into a "work camp" many months ago. A United States Army unit had saved them. And the officer wanted to escort the grandparents to their family in America.

Alex and Emmy forgot about the presents under the tree. The only presents they cared about were now here, Grandma and Grandpa, at home where they belonged.

Dudley had done a great job this Christmas. His landing was perfect. And with the wave of his wand, he brought a miracle and proved that love is the best Christmas gift of all.

Dudley did not really know how powerful his mission was. He put together a family who thought they were broken. Miracles happen and cannot be explained.

Dudley's mission was bigger than anyone thought. He brought six hearts together in a new home, in their new country.

An angel's perfect landing makes miracles happen. An angel's perfect flight turns "Nothing" into "Everything."

Chapter 6
Friends

Hello, children, it's Gabby.

Quite a story, huh? There are so many things to think about.

- ✓ Angels, elves, and falling Christmas balls

- ✓ Dudley's golden wings

- ✓ The family's Christmas miracle

What was your favorite part? As you get older, your answer might change.

Someday if you have children or even grandchildren, the Christmas balls will fall off your tree. Maybe you will remember us and have a happy thought about your friends Dudley and Gabby, Alex, Emmy, Momma, Poppa, Grandma, and Grandpa. We will never forget you!

Hold on, hold on. I have a call coming in. It is from Dudley.

"Dudley … what? … I know you made the perfect landing and you have your golden wings … Yes. I know you are a hero … No, I didn't pull your ears …

"Yes, we should call that cute little angel and elf that we met down at the convention last year. Yes, good idea. Yes, a little Christmas party. Yes, but don't tell your mother.

"What? … Yes, Dudley. I will tell them. … Yes, I will tell them from both of us. I will tell all the children and all who love them …"

MERRY CHRISTMAS!

And to all a good "flight!"

Printed in the United States
by Baker & Taylor Publisher Services